Psychology Series

ALFRED ADLER

HUMAN DESPICABLENESS

gece
kitaplığı

İmtiyaz Sahibi / Publisher • Yaşar Hız

Genel Yayın Yönetmeni / Editor in Chief • Eda Altunel

Kapak & İç Tasarım / Cover & Interior Design • Karaf Ajans

Birinci Basım / First Edition • © TEMMUZ 2020

ISBN • 978-625-7836-41-8

Gece Kitaplığı / Gece Publishing

Türkiye Adres / Turkey Address: Kızılay Mah. Fevzi Çakmak 1.
Sokak

Ümit Apt. No: 22/A Çankaya / Ankara / TR

Telefon / Phone: +90 312 384 80 40

web: www.gecekitapligi.com

e-mail: gecekitapligi@gmail.com

Baskı & Cilt / Printing & Volume

Sertifika / Certificate No: 47083

Psychology Series

ALFRED ADLER

HUMAN DESPICABLENESS

THE FEELING OF INFERIORITY AND THE STRIVING FOR RECOGNITION

I. The situation in early childhood

We are now certainly prepared to recognize the fact that children who have been treated as step-children by Nature have an entirely different attitude toward life and toward their fellow human beings than those to whom the joys of existence were vouchsafed at an early age. One can state as a fundamental law that children who come into the world with organ inferiorities become involved at an early age in a bitter struggle for existence which results only too often in the strangulation of their social feelings. Instead of interesting themselves in an adjustment to their fellows, they are continually preoccupied with themselves, and with the impression which they make on others. What holds good for an organic inferiority is as valid for any social or economic burden which might manifest itself as an additional load, capable of producing a hostile attitude toward the world. The deciding trend becomes determined at an early age. Such children frequently have a sentiment as early as their second year of life, that they are somehow not as adequately equipped for the struggle as their playmates; they sense that they dare not trust themselves to the common games and pastimes. As a result of past privations, they have acquired a feeling of being neglected, which is expressed in their attitude of anxious expectation. One must remember that every child occupies an inferior position in life; were it not for a certain quantum of social feeling on the part of his family he would be incapable of independent existence. One realizes that the beginning of every life is fraught with a more or less deep feeling of inferiority when one sees the weakness and helplessness of every child. Sooner or later every child becomes conscious of his inability to cope single-handed with the challenges of existence. This feeling of inferiority is the driving force, the starting point from which every childish striving originates. It determines how this individual child acquires peace and security in life, it determines the very goal of his existence, and prepares the path along which this goal may be reached.

The basis of a child's educability lies in this peculiar situation which is so closely bound up with his organic potentialities. Educability may be shattered by two factors. One of these factors is an exaggerated, intensified, unresolved feeling of inferiority, and the other is a goal which demands not only security and peace and social equilibrium, but a striving to express power over the environment, a goal of dominance over one's fellows. Children who have such a goal are always easily recognized. They become "problem" children because they interpret every experience as a defeat, and because they consider themselves always neglected and discriminated against both by nature and by man. One need but consider all these factors to see with what compulsive necessity a crooked, inadequate, error-ridden development may occur in the life of a child. Every child runs the danger of a mistaken development. Every child finds itself in a situation which is precarious, at some time or another.

Since every child must grow up in an environment of adults he is predisposed to consider himself weak, small, incapable of living alone; he does not trust himself to do these simple tasks that one thinks him capable of doing, without mistakes, errors, or clumsinesses. Most of our errors in education begin at this point. In demanding more than the child can do, the idea of his own helplessness is thrown into his face. Some children are even consciously made to feel their smallness and helplessness. Other children are regarded as toys, as animated dolls; others, again, are treated as valuable property that must be carefully watched, white others still are made to feel they are so much useless human freight. A combination of these attitudes on the part of the parents and adults often leads a child to believe that there are but two thinks in his power, the pleasure or displeasure of his elders. The type of inferiority feeling produced by the parents may be further intensified by certain peculiar characteristics of our civilization. The habit of not taking children seriously belongs in this category. A child gets the impression that he is a nobody, without rights; that he is to be seen, not heard, that he must be courteous, quiet, and the like.

Numerous children grow up in the constant dread of being laughed at. Ridicule of children is well-nigh criminal. It retains its effect upon the soul of the child and is transferred into the habits and actions of his adulthood. An adult who was continually laughed at as a child may be easily recognized; he cannot rid himself of the fear of being made ridiculous again. Another aspect of this matter of not taking children seriously is the custom of telling children palpable lies, with the result that the child begins to doubt not only his immediate environment but also to question the seriousness and reality of life.

Cases have been recorded of children who laughed continually at school, seemingly without reason, who when questioned, admitted that they thought school was one of their parents' jokes and not worth taking seriously!

II. Compensating for the feeling of inferiority; the striving for recognition and superiority

It is the feeling of inferiority, inadequacy, insecurity, which determines the goal of an individual's existence. The tendency to push into the limelight, to compel the attention of parents, makes itself felt in the first days of life. Here are found the first indications of the awakening desire for recognition developing itself under the concomitant influence of the sense of inferiority, with its purpose the attainment of a goal in which the individual is seemingly superior to his environment.

The degree and quality of the social feeling helps to determine the goal of dominance We cannot judge any individual, whether it is a child or adult, without drawing a comparison between his goal of personal dominance and the quantum of his social feeling. His goal is so constructed that its achievement promises the possibility either of a sentiment of superiority, or an elevation of the personality to such a degree that life seems worth living. It is this goal which gives value to our sensations, which links and coordinates our sentiments, which shapes our imagination and directs our creative powers, determines what we shall remember and what we must forget. We can realize how relative are the values of sensations, sentiments, affects, and imagination, when not even these are absolute quantities; these elements of our psychic activity are influenced by the striving for a definite goal, our very perceptions are prejudiced by it, and are chosen, so to speak, with a secret hint at the final goal toward which the personality is striving.

We orient ourselves according to a fixed point which we have artificially created, which does not in reality exist, a fiction. This assumption is necessary because of the inadequacy of our psychic life. It is very similar to other fictions which are used in other sciences, such as the division of the earth by nonexistent, but highly useful meridians. In the case of all psychic fictions we have to do with the following: we assume a fixed point even though closer observation forces us to admit that it does not exist. The purpose of this assumption is simply to orient ourselves in the chaos of existence, so that we can arrive at some apperception of relative values. The advantage is that we can categorize every sensation and every sentiment according to this fixed point, once we have assumed it.

Individual Psychology, therefore, creates for itself a heuristic system and method: to regard human behavior and understand it as though a final constellation of relationships were produced under the influence of the striving for a definite goal upon the basic inherited potentialities of the organism. Our experience, however, has shown us that the assumption of a striving for a goal is more than simply a convenient fiction. It has shown itself to be largely coincident with the actual facts in its fundamentals, whether these facts are to be found in the conscious or unconscious life. The striving for a goal, the purposiveness of the psychic life is not only a philosophic assumption, but actually a fundamental fact.

When we question how we can most advantageously oppose the development of the striving for power, this most prominent evil of our civilization, we are faced with a difficulty, for this striving begins when the child cannot be easily approached. One can begin to make attempts at improvement and clarification only much later in life. But *living* with the child at this time does offer an opportunity to so develop his social feeling that the striving for personal power becomes a negligible factor.

A further difficulty lies in the fact that children do not express their striving for power openly but hide it under the guise of charity and tenderness, and carry out their work behind a veil. Modestly, they expect to escape disclosure in this way. An uninhibited striving for power is capable of producing degenerations in the psychic development of the child, an exaggerated drive for security and might, may change courage to impudence, obedience into cowardice, tenderness into a subtle treachery for dominating the world. Every natural feeling or expression finally carries with it a hypocritical afterthought whose final purpose is the subjugation of the environment.

Education affects the child by virtue of its conscious or unconscious desire to compensate him for his insecurity, by schooling him in the technique of life, by giving him an educated understanding, and by furnishing him with a social feeling for his fellows. All these measures, whatever their source, are means to help the growing child rid himself of his insecurity and his feeling of inferiority. What happens in the soul of the child during this process we must judge by the character traits he develops since these are the mirror of the activity in his soul. The actual inferiority of a child, important as it is for his psychic economy, is no criterion of the weight of his feeling of insecurity and inferiority, since these depend largely upon his interpretation of them.

One cannot expect a child to have a correct estimation of himself in any particular situation; one does not expect it of adults! It is precisely here that difficulties grow apace. One child will grow up in a situation so complicated that errors concerning the degree of his inferiority are absolutely unavoidable. Another child will be able better to interpret his situation. But taken by and large the interpretation which the child has of his feeling of inferiority varies from day to day until it becomes consolidated, finally, and is expressed as a definite self-estimation; this becomes a "constant" of self-evaluation which the child retains, in all his conduct. According to this crystallized norm or "constant of self-estimation" the compensation trends which the child creates to guide him out of his inferiority will be directed toward this, or the other, goal.

The mechanism of the striving for compensation with which the soul attempts to neutralize the tortured feeling of inferiority has its analogy in the organic world. It is a well-known fact that those organs of our body which are essential for life, produce an overgrowth, and over function when their productivity is lessened through damage to their normal state. Thus, in difficulties of circulation, the heart, seeming to draw its new strength from the whole body, may enlarge until it is more powerful than a normal heart. Similarly, the soul, under pressure of the feeling of inferiority, or the torturing thought that the individual is small and helpless, attempts with all its might to become master over this "inferiority complex."

When the feeling of inferiority is intensified to the degree that the child fears he will never be able to compensate for his weakness, the danger arises that in his striving for compensation he will be satisfied not with a simple restoration of the balance of power; he will demand an overcompensation, will seek an overbalance of the scales!

The striving for power and dominance may become so exaggerated and intensified that it must be called pathological. When this occurs the ordinary relationships of life will never be satisfactory. The movements in these cases are apt to have a certain grandiose gesture about them. They are well adapted to their goal. Where we are dealing with pathological power-drive we find individuals who seek to secure their position in life with extraordinary efforts, with greater haste and impatience, with more violent impulses, and without consideration of anyone else. These are the children whose actions become more noticeable because of their exaggerated movements towards their exaggerated goal of dominance; their attacks on the lives of others necessitate that they defend their own lives. They are against the world, and the world is against them.

This need not necessarily occur in the worst sense of the word. There are children who express the striving of power in a manner not calculated to bring them into immediate conflict with society, and their ambition may be considered as no abnormal characteristic. Yet when we carefully investigate their activity and achievements, we find that society at large does not benefit from their triumphs, because their ambition is an asocial one. Their ambition will always put them in the path of other human beings as disturbing elements. Little by little, too, other characteristics will appear which, if we consider total human relationships, will assume an increasingly antisocial color.

In the forefront of these manifestations are pride, vanity, and the desire to conquer everyone at any price. The latter may be subtly accomplished by the relative elevation of the individual, by his deprecation of all those with whom he comes in contact. In the latter case the important thing is the "distance" which separates him from his fellows. His attitude is not only uncomfortable for the environment, but for the individual who practices it, because it continually brings him into contact with the dank side of life and prevents him from experiencing any joy in living.

The exaggerated drive for power with which some children wish to assure their prestige over their environment, soon forces them into an attitude of resistance against the ordinary tasks and duties of everyday life. Compare such a power hungry individual with the ideal social being, and one can, after some little experience, specify, so to speak, his social index, that is, the degree to which he has removed himself from his fellow man. A keen judge of human nature, keeping his eyes open to the value of physical defects and inferiorities, knows nevertheless that such character traits were impossible without antecedent difficulties in the evolution of his soul.

When we have gained a true knowledge of human nature, built upon a recognition of the value of the difficulties which may occur in the proper development of the soul, it can never be an instrument of harm so long as we have ourselves thoroughly developed our social feeling. We can but help our fellow men with it. We must not blame the bearer of a physical defect, nor a disagreeable character trait, for his indignation. He is not responsible for it. We must indeed admit his right to be indignant to the last limits, and we must be conscious that we bear a part of the common blame for his situation. The blame belongs to us because we too have taken part in the inadequate precautions against the social misery which has produced it. If we stick to this standpoint, we can eventually ameliorate the situation.

We approach such an individual not as a degraded, worthless outcast, but as a fellow human being; we give him an atmosphere in which he will find that there are possibilities for feeling himself the equal of every other human being in his environment. Think how unpleasant the sight of an individual's appearance, whose organ or bodily inferiorities are externally visible, may be to you! It is a good index of the amount of education you yourself need in order to come to an absolutely just sense of social values, and put yourself into complete harmony with the truth of the social feeling. And we can judge then, too, how much our civilization owes to such an individual.

It is self-understood that those who come into the world with organ inferiorities feel an added burden of existence from their earliest days, and, as a result, find themselves pessimistic as regards the whole matter of existence. Children in whom the feeling of inferiority has become intensified through some cause or other, although their organ inferiorities are not nearly so noticeable, find themselves in a similar situation. The feeling of inferiority may be so intensified artificially that the result is exactly the same as though the child came into the world greatly crippled. A very severe education during the critical period, for instance, may affect such an unfortunate result. The thorn which has been stuck into their side in the early days of their existence is never removed, and the coldness which they have experienced prevents them from approaching other human beings in their environment. They believe themselves thus in a world devoid of love and affection, with which they have no common point of contact.

An example: A patient, noticeable because he is continually telling us about his great sense of duty, and the importance of all his actions, lives with his wife in the worst possible relationship. Here are two individuals who measure the value of any event as a means toward the subjugation of their mate, to the thickness of a hair. Wrangling, reproaches, insults, in the course of which the two become entirely estranged from one another, are the inevitable result. What little social feeling for his fellow men the husband retains, at least as far as his wife and friends are concerned, is choked by his thirst for superiority.

We learn the following facts from the story of his life: - he was practically undeveloped physically until his seventeenth year. His voice was the voice of a young boy, he had no body or face hair, and he was among the smallest boys in his school. Today he is thirty-six. Nothing which is not entirely masculine is noticeable about his outer appearance, and Nature seemingly has caught up with herself and completed everything which she had hardly begun to fashion when he was seventeen. But for eight years he suffered from this failure of development, and at that time he had no guarantee that Nature would ever compensate for his anomalies. During this entire period, he was tortured with the thought that he must always remain a "child."

At that early age the beginnings of his present character traits could be noted. He acted as though he were very important, and as if his every action had the utmost weight. Every movement served the purpose of bringing him into the center of attention. In the course of time he acquired those characteristics which we see in him today. After he married he was continually occupied with impressing his wife with the fact that he was really bigger and more important than she thought, while she was continually busied with showing him that his assertions concerning his value were untrue! Under these circumstances their marriage, which showed signs of disruption even during their engagement, could hardly develop favorably, and ended finally in a social cataclysm. The patient came to the physician at this time—since the break-up of his marriage served only to accentuate the dilapidation of his already battered self-esteem. To be cured, he had to learn first from the physician how to know human nature, he had to learn how to appreciate the error he had made in life. And this error, this wrong evaluation of his inferiority, had colored his entire life up to the time of his treatment.

III. The graph of life and the cosmic picture

When we demonstrate cases like these it is frequently convenient to show relationships between the childhood impressions and the actual complaint, as presented by the patient; this is best done by a graph, similar to a mathematical formula. A line connecting two points represents such an equation. We will succeed in many cases in being able to plot this graph of life, the spiritual curve along which the entire movement of an individual has taken place. The equation of the curve is the behavior pattern which this individual has followed since earliest childhood. Perhaps there will be some readers who have the impression that we are attempting to belittle human fate by oversimplifying it, or that we have a tendency to, deny that every human being is the master of his life, and that we are denying free will and judgment. So far as free will is concerned this accusation is true. Actually we see this behavior pattern, whose final configuration is subject to some few changes, but whose essential content, whose energy and meaning, remain unchanged from earliest childhood, is the determining factor, even though the relations to the adult environment which follow the childhood situation may tend to modify it in some instances. In our examination we must ferret out the history of the earliest childhood days, because the impressions of early infancy indicate the direction in which a child has developed, as well as the direction in which he will respond in the future to the challenge of existence. In his response to the challenge of existence a child will utilize all the developed mental possibilities he has brought with him into life; the particular pressure he has felt in the days of earliest infancy will color his attitude toward life and determine in a primitive fashion his world-view, his cosmic philosophy.

It should not surprise us to learn that people do not change their attitude toward life after their infancy, though its expressions in later life are quite different from those of their earliest days. It is important therefore to put an infant into relationships in which it will be difficult for him to assume a false concept of life. The strength and resistance of his body is an important factor in this process. His social position, and the characteristics of those who educate him, are almost equally important. Even though the response to life is automatic and reflex in the beginning, type reactions become modified according to a certain purposiveness, in later life. In the beginning the factors of personal necessity condition his pain and his happiness, but later he acquires the ability to evade and circumvent the pressure of these primitive needs. This phenomenon occurs in the time of self-discovery, approximately during the time that a child begins to speak of himself as "I". It is during this time also that the child is already conscious that he stands in a fixed relationship to his environment. This relationship is by no means neutral, since it forces the child to assume a different attitude and to adjust his relationships according to the demands which his worldview, and his conception of happiness and completeness, give him.

If we reaffirm what has been said concerning the teleology of the psychic life of mankind it will become increasingly clear to us that an indestructible unity must be a special token of this behavior pattern. The necessity for treating with a human being only as unit personality becomes increasingly clear in those cases where seemingly contrasting expressions of psychic trends are to be found. There are children whose behavior at school and at home are diametrically opposite to one another, just as there are adults whose character traits appear so contradictory that we are deceived concerning their true character. In the same way the movements and expressions of two human beings may be outwardly identical, yet when examined for their underlying behavior patterns, prove themselves to be entirely different. When two individuals seem to be doing the same thing, each one is really doing something distinct and different, yet when two individuals are doing seemingly different things, they may actually be doing the same thing!

Because of this possibility of many meanings we can never judge the expressions of the psychic life as single isolated phenomena; on the contrary, we must evaluate them according to the unit goal toward which they are directed. The essential meaning can be learned only when we know what value a phenomenon has in the entire context of a person's life. We can have an understanding of his psychic life only when we have reaffirmed the law that every expression of a man's life is an aspect of his unit behavior pattern.

When we have finally comprehended that all human behavior is based upon the striving for a goal, that it is conditioned by its end as well as by its beginning, then we can comprehend also wherein lies the possibility of the greatest mistakes. The source of these errors lies in the fact that every one of us utilizes his triumphs and psychic assets according to his particular pattern, and in the sense of a reinforcement of his individual life pattern. This is possible only because we do not test anything, but receive, transform, and assimilate all perceptions in the shadow of our own conscious, or the depths of our unconscious. Science alone can illuminate the process and make it comprehensible; science alone is finally able to modify it. We shall conclude our exposition at this point with an example in which we will analyze and explain every phenomenon by those Individual Psychological concepts which we have already learned.

A young woman comes as a patient and complains of her unconquerable dissatisfaction with life, which arises, as she believes, in the fact that her whole day is taken up with a great number of duties of all kinds.

Externally we can see in her a hasty being, with restless eyes, who complains of the great unrest which seizes her whenever she must do some simple duty. From her family and friends, we learn that she takes everything seriously and seems to be breaking under the burden of her work. The general impression that we get is that of a person who takes everything very seriously, a characteristic which is common to many people. One member of her family gives us the clue in saying, "She is always making a big fuss over everything!"

Let us test this tendency to consider every simple task a particularly hard and important one, by attempting to imagine what kind of an impression this behavior would make upon a group of people, or in the marriage relationship. We cannot help feeling that such a tendency simulates an appeal to the environment not to forte any further work upon her since she can no longer do the most elementary tasks.

Our knowledge of this woman's personality is not yet adequate. We must stimulate her to further expressions of herself. One must proceed by innuendo and with the proper delicacy in such examinations. There must be no attempt to dominate the patient as this would only serve to make her belligerent. Once her confidence is won and the possibility of conversation is given, we come to the conclusion that her whole being is concerned with but a single goal. Her behavior shows that she is attempting to demonstrate to someone, probably her husband, that she cannot bear any further obligations or responsibilities, that she must be treated carefully and with tenderness. We can further suspect and imagine that all this must have begun definitely at some time in the past, and that such demands must have been made of her. We succeed in stimulating her to the affirmation that many years ago she had to live through a period in which nothing was more wanting than tenderness. Now we can understand her behavior better; it is a reinforcement of her desire for consideration, and an attempt to prevent the recurrence of a situation in which her hunger for warmth and affection might somehow remain unsatisfied.

Our findings are clinched by a further explanation on her part. She tells of a friend who is in many ways her opposite, who is living in an unhappy marriage from which she desires to escape. Once she met her friend at a moment when she was standing, book in hand, telling her husband in a bored voice that she really did not know whether she would be able to prepare dinner that day. This irritated her husband so that he criticized her whole personality in harsh terms. To this occurrence our patient added: "When I think of this occurrence, I think that my method is much better. No one can reproach me in this way because I am overburdened with work from morning until night. If a luncheon is not prepared on time at my house no one can say anything to me because my time is full of haste and constant excitement. Should I give up this method now?"

One can understand what is going on in this soul. In a relatively innocuous way, she attempts to attain a certain superiority, but remain at the same time beyond every reproach by pleading constantly for tender treatment. Since this mechanism is successful it seems hardly reasonable to ask her to forego it, but there is more to her behavior than just this. Her appeal for tenderness (which at the same time is an attempt to dominate others) can never be made drastic enough. Contradictions of all kinds occur in this connection, should anything be lost in the house there is a consequent "much ado about nothing"; subsequently she has so much business that she is constantly suffering from headaches, and she can never sleep quietly because she is under the necessity of putting her activities in the right light. An invitation which she may get is in itself an important occasion. Enormous preparations are necessary for its acceptance. Since the least activity appears to her inordinately large, paying a call is a difficult labor which demands hours and days to complete. We can predict with some certainty that she will either send her regrets or, at the very least, come late. The social feeling in the life of such a person can never go beyond certain limits.

In married life there are a number of relationships which assume a peculiar significance through this appeal for tenderness. It is conceivable for instance that a husband must be absent because of his business, or that he must make visits by himself, or that he must appear at meetings of societies to which he belongs. If he left his wife at home at these times would this not be a breach of tenderness and consideration? At first we might say, and very often this is the case, marriage justifies keeping a husband at home as much as possible. Pleasant as this obligation might seem in part, in actuality it signifies insupportable difficulties for any man who has a profession. Disharmony would appear unavoidable in such cases and it occurred quickly in this one. The husband attempted occasionally to come to his bed Tate at night without disturbing his wife only to be surprised to find her still awake, greeting him with reproachful glances.

We need not picture here all the well-known situations of this kind. Nor should we overlook the fact that it is not alone the petty vices of women which we are discussing, for there are as many men whole attitude is similar. We are simply concerned with showing that the demand for especial consideration may occasionally take a different course. In our case the following procedure would occur: If on some occasion the husband has to spend an evening out, his wife tells him that since he goes into society so seldom, he should not come home too early. Although she says this in a jocular tone her words have very serious meaning. It seems to negate the previous impression but when we observe more closely, we can see the connection. The wife is clever enough not to act too strictly. Outwardly she is utterly charming. There is no blemish upon her character, and she interests us only in a psychological way. The real significance of her words to her husband lies in the fact that it is the *wife* who has given an ultimatum. Now since *she* has permitted it, he may stay out late whereas she would be dreadfully hurt and slighted if he had remained away for reasons of his own. Her words drape a veil over the whole situation. She has become the directing partner; and her husband, even though he is only fulfilling his social obligations, is made dependent upon the wish and will of his wife.

Now let us connect this hunger for particular tenderness with our newly won concept that this woman can bear a situation only when she herself commands. We suddenly become aware that throughout her whole life she has been actuated by an impulse never to play the second fiddle, always to maintain her dominancy, never to be thrust from her secure Position by any reproach, and always to remain in the center of her little environment. We will find this movement in every situation in which we find her; for instance, when she has to get a new maid, she becomes highly excited. Clearly, she is concerned to know whether she will be able to maintain the same dominance over the new servant that she was able to hold over the old. In like manner, when she is about to leave the house for a walk, she leaves a sphere where her dominance is unconditionally secure, and goes out into the world, on the street where suddenly nothing is under the shadow of her dominance, where she has to dodge every automobile, indeed where she plays a very subordinate role. The cause and meaning of her tension become perfectly clear when one can understand what tyranny she exercises at home.

These characteristics may often appear in such a pleasant pattern that at the first glance one would never think that the person was suffering. On the other hand, this suffering can reach a very high degree. Just imagine this tension exaggerated and enlarged. There are human beings who are afraid of using a streetcar because in a streetcar they are not the masters of their own will and this may go so far that they finally do not leave their homes at all.

A further development in our case is an instructive example of the influence which childhood impressions exercise in the life of an individual. We cannot deny the fact that this woman, from her standpoint, is perfectly right; if one's attitude, and one's whole life are directed with unheard of intensity toward the acquisition of warmth, respect, honor, and tenderness, then to act as though one were constantly overloaded and constantly exhausted is not a bad means to this end. No other way will always serve to keep off criticism, and simultaneously force the environment to be gentle, and avoid everything likely to disturb a wavering psychic equilibrium.

If we go back a considerable period in the life of our patient we learn that even in school, whenever she could not do her homework, she became extraordinarily excited and forced her teacher in this way to be very gentle with her. To this she adds, she was the oldest of three children and was followed by a boy and then by a sister. She was constantly at war with her brother. He always appeared as the preferred one. She angered herself especially because people paid more attention to his schoolwork, whereas her work (and she had originally been a good pupil) was met with a certain indifference as to her accomplishments. Finally, she could hardly bear it any longer and was forever nagging to know why her accomplishments were not judged of equal value.

Thus, we can understand that this young girl was striving for equality, and that from earliest childhood she had had a Feeling of inferiority which she was attempting to overcome. Her compensation in school was made in such a manner that she became a bad pupil. She attempted to outdo her brother by means of bad school reports! These are no high ethics, but in her childish interpretation she acted rationally, for the attention of her parents would be more often directed to her in this way. Some of her tricks must have been conscious because she declared quite clearly that she *wanted* to be a bad pupil!

Her parents, however, did not trouble themselves in the least about her failures in school. And now something interesting happened. She suddenly showed marked success in her studies, for now her younger sister entered upon the scene in a new role! This younger sister also had failed in school but her mother troubled herself almost as much about her failure as she had about the brother, and for the peculiar reason that whereas our patient had had bad reports only in her studies her sister got bad reports in conduct and behavior. She was thus able to gain her mother's attention more easily since bad reports in conduct have an entirely different social effect than merely bad reports in studies. They were bound up with peculiar emergencies that forced the parents to occupy themselves more with their child.

The battle for equality was temporarily lost. Now the loss of a battle for equality never leads to a permanent peace. No human being can bear such a situation. Hence, we shall constantly find new tendencies and activities contributing toward the formation of her character. We can now understand the meaning of her great to-do, her constant haste, her desire to show herself under pressure, somewhat better. It was meant originally for her mother and was intended to compel her parents' attention to her as well as to her brother and sister; at the same time it was a reproach to her parents that they treated her worse than the others. The fundamental attitude created at that time has remained until today.

We can go back even farther in her life. She remembers as a particularly vivid occurrence of her childhood, that she wanted to hit her brother who had just been born, with a piece of wood, and that only the care of her mother had prevented her from doing great damage. At this time, she was three years old. This little girl had discovered (even at that time) the cause for her neglect and lesser evaluation was that she was only a girl. She remembers quite vividly that the wish to be a boy was expressed countless times. The arrival of her brother not only forced her out of the warmth of her nest, but she was particularly insulted because as a boy he was treated much better than she had ever been. In her striving to compensate for this defect she happened upon the method of appearing always overloaded with work.

Let us interpret a dream now to show how deeply this behavior pattern is anchored in the soul. This woman dreamt that she was at home conversing with her husband, but her husband did not look like a man but appeared as a woman. This detail is symbolic of the pattern with which she approaches all her experiences and all her relationships. The dream means that she has found equality with her husband. He is no longer the dominant male as her brother once was, he is already like a woman. There is no difference in elevation between them. In her dream she has achieved that which she has always wished since her childhood.

In this way we have succeeded in joining two points in the soul life of a human being. We have discovered her style of life, her life curve, her behavior pattern, and from this we can acquire a unified picture which we might sum up as follows: we are dealing here with a human being who strive& to play the dominant role by amiable means.

THE PREPARATION FOR LIFE

One of the fundamental tenets of Individual Psychology is that all the psychic phenomena can be considered as preparations for a definite goal. In the configuration of the soul life which we have previously described we can see a constant preparation for the future in which the wishes of the individual appear fulfilled. This is a general human experience and all of us must go through this process. All the myths, legends and sagas which speak of an ideal future state concern themselves with it. The convictions of all peoples that there was once a paradise, and the further echo of this process in the desire of humanity for a future in which all difficulties have been overcome, may be found in all religions. The dogma of the immortality of the soul, or its reincarnation, is a definite evidence of the belief that the soul can arrive at a new configuration. Every fairy tale is a witness of the fact that the hope of a happy future has never failed in mankind.

I. Play

There is in the child life an important phenomenon which shows very clearly the process of preparation for the future. It is play. Games are not to be considered as haphazard ideas of parents or educators, but they are to be considered as educational aids and as stimuli for the spirit, for the fantasy, and for the life-technique of the child. The preparation for the future can be seen in every game. The manner in which a child approaches a game, his choice, and the importance which he places upon it, indicate his attitude and relationship to his environment and how he is related to his fellow men. whether he is hostile or whether he is friendly, and particularly whether he has the tendency to be a ruler, is evident in his play; and in observing a child in his play we can see his whole attitude toward life. Play is of utmost importance to every child. The discovery of these facts which teach us that the play of children is to be considered as a preparation for the future is due to Gross, a professor of pedagogy, who discovered the same tendencies in the play of animals.

But we have not exhausted all the viewpoints as to the nature of play, with the concept of preparation. Above all else games are communal exercises; they enable the child to satisfy and fulfill his social feeling. Children who evade games and play are always open to the suspicion that they have made a bad adjustment to life. These children gladly withdraw themselves from all games, or when they are put on the playground with other children usually spoil the pleasure of the others. Pride, deficient self-esteem and the consequent fear of playing one's role badly are the chief reasons for this behavior. In general, by watching a child at play we shall be able to determine with great certainty the quantum of his social feeling.

The goal of superiority, another factor obvious in play, betrays itself in the child's tendency to be the commander and the ruler. We can discover this tendency by watching how the child pushes himself forward and to what degree he prefers those games which give him an opportunity to satisfy his desire to play the leading role. There are very few games which do not have at least one of these factors, preparation for life, social feeling, or the striving for domination, incorporated in them.

There is, however, one other factor which is present in play. It is the possibility that the child can express himself in a game. The child is more or less placed upon his own in play, and his performance is stimulated by his connection with the other children. There are a number of games which especially emphasize this creative bent. In the preparation for a future profession those plays which carry in themselves the possibility for the exercise of the creative spirit of the child are especially important. In the life histories of many people, it has happened that they have made dresses for dolls in their childhood, and later made dresses for adults.

Play is indivisibly connected with the soul. It is, so to speak, a kind of profession, and must be considered as such. Therefore, it is not an insignificant matter to disturb a child in his play. Play should never be considered as a method of killing time. In regard to the goal of preparing for the future, every child has in him something of the adult he will be at some time. Thus, in the appraisal of an individual we can draw our conclusions more easily when we have a knowledge of his childhood.

II. Attention and distraction

Attention is one of the characteristics of the soul which is in the very forefront of human accomplishments. When we bring our sense organs to the consideration of some particular event outside or inside our person, we have a feeling of particular tension, which does not spread over our entire body, but is limited to a single sense organ, as for instance, the eye. We have the feeling that something is being prepared. In the case of the eye the direction of the ocular axis gives us this particular feeling of tension.

If attention calls forth a particular tension in any part of the soul or in our motor organism, then other tensions are at the same time excluded. Thus, as soon as we wish to be attentive to any one thing, we desire to exclude all other disturbances. Attention, so far as the soul is concerned, means an attitude of willingness to make a special bridge between ourselves and a definite fact, a preparation for offense, which grows out of our necessity, or out of an unusual situation which demands that our whole power be directed toward a particular purpose.

Every human being, if we exclude sickness and feeblemindedness, possesses the ability to pay attention, but inattentive persons are frequently found. There are a number of reasons for this. In the first place, fatigue or sickness are factors which influence the ability to pay attention. Further, there are other individuals whose deficient attention is due to the fact that they do not want to pay attention, because the object to which they should be attentive does not fit into their behavior pattern; on the other hand their attention immediately awakens when they are considering some matter which is germane to their style of life. A further reason for deficient attention is to be found in the tendency toward opposition. Children are very easily given to opposition, and it often happens that such children answer "No" to every stimulus which is offered them. It is necessary for their opposition to become open. It is the duty of the educator and of educational tact to reconcile such a child by relating the study which he must learn to his behavior pattern and making it germane to his style of life.

Some see and hear and perceive every change. Some approach life entirely with their eyes; others entirely with their auditory apparatus. Some see nothing, take notice of nothing, and are not to be interested in visual things. We may find an individual inattentive when his situation would warrant his utmost interest because his more sensitive receptors are not stimulated.

The most important factor in the awakening of attention is a really deep-rooted interest in the world. Interest lies in a much deeper psychic stratum than attention. If we have interest, then it is self-understood that we should also pay attention; and where interest exists, an educator need not concern himself with attention. It becomes a simple instrument with which one conquers a field of knowledge for a definite purpose. No one has ever developed without making mistakes in the process. It follows that the attention is likewise involved when some such mistaken attitude has become fixed in an individual, and it thus happens that attention is directed toward things which are not important in the preparation for life. When the *interest* is directed towards one's own body, or towards one's own power, one is *attentive* wherever these interests become involved, wherever there is something to be won, or wherever one's power is threatened. Attention can never be linked with something extraneous so long as some new interest is not substituted in place of the power interest. One can observe how children become immediately attentive when their recognition and significance are in question. Their attention on the other hand is easily extinguished when they have the feeling there is "nothing in it" for them.

A defective attention actually means nothing more than that a person prefers to withdraw from a situation, to which he is supposed to pay attention. It is incorrect, therefore, to say that someone cannot concentrate himself. It can easily be proved that he concentrates very well, but always on something else. Lack of will power and lack of energy are similar to the inability to concentrate. We usually find an obdurate will and an indomitable energy expressed in a different direction in these cases. Treatment is not simple. It can be attempted solely by changing the entire style of life of the individual. In every case we can be sure that we are dealing with a defect only because another goal is being pursued.

Not infrequently inattention becomes a permanent characteristic. We often meet individuals who have been given a definite task which they have declined to do, which they have only partially accomplished, or have fully evaded, with the result that they are always a burden to someone else. Their constant inattention is a fixed character trait, which appears as soon as they are under the necessity of doing something which is demanded of them.

III. Criminal negligence and forgetfulness

We usually speak of criminal negligence when the safety or health of an individual is threatened by neglect in the application of necessary precaution. Criminal neglect is a phenomenon which demonstrates the utmost degree of inattention. Such defective attention is based on a defective interest for one's fellow men. One can determine whether children think only of themselves, or whether they take into consideration rights of others, by watching for traits of negligence in their games. Such phenomena are definite standards of the communal consciousness and the social feeling of a human being. When the social feeling has been insufficiently developed, one acquires sufficient interest for his fellows only with the greatest difficulty, even under threat of punishment; whereas in the presence of a well-developed community consciousness, this interest is self-evident.

Criminal neglect, therefore, amounts to a defective social feeling, yet we must not be too intolerant lest we forget to investigate why an individual does not possess the interest in his fellow men which we might expect of him.

We can produce forgetfulness by setting limits to our attention, just as we can arrange the loss of valuables. Despite the presence of the possibility for greater tension—that is, interest —this interest may be so dampened by displeasure, that a loss or memory lapse is initiated, or at least facilitated thereby. Such is the case, for instance, when children lose their schoolbooks. It is always easy to prove that they have not yet become accustomed to their school surroundings. Housewives who are constantly losing or misplacing their keys are usually women who have never become friendly with their profession as housewife. Forgetful people usually prefer not to revolt openly, yet a certain lack of interest in their tasks is betrayed by their forgetfulness.

IV. The unconscious

Our descriptions have often shown individuals who are not conscious of the meaning of the phenomena of their psychic life. Seldom will an attentive man be able to tell you why he sees everything at once. Certain psychic faculties are not to be sought in the realm of consciousness; although we can consciously force our attention to a certain degree, the stimulus to that attention lies not in consciousness, but in our interests, and these, again, lie for the most part in the sphere of the unconscious. Taken in its largest scope, this is at once an aspect and an important factor in the soul life. We may seek and find the behavior pattern of a man in the unconscious. In his conscious life we have but a reflection, a negative, to deal with. A vain woman usually has no knowledge of her vanity in most of the instances in which she exhibits it; quite to the contrary, she will behave so that only her modesty will be apparent to everyone. It is not necessary to know that one is vain to be vain. Indeed, for the purposes of this woman, it would be quite futile for her to know that she is vain, since if she knew she were vain, she could not continue to be vain. We can acquire a certain dramatic security in not seeing anything of our own vanity solely by directing our attention to something extraneous or irrelevant. The whole process takes place in the dark. Attempt to talk to a vain man about his vanity and you will find it very difficult to achieve a conversation on the subject. He may show a tendency to evade the matter, to circumlocute, lest he be disturbed; this can but make us more certain of our opinion. He wants to play his little game, and immediately assumes a defensive attitude when someone inadvertently attempts to lift the veil from his little trick.

Human beings may be differentiated into two types; those who know more concerning their unconscious life than the average, and those who know less; that is, according to the extent of their sphere of consciousness. In a great many cases, we will find coincidentally that an individual of the second type concentrates upon a small sphere of activity, whereas the individuals of the first type are connected with a many-sided sphere, and have large interests in men, things, events, and ideas. Those individuals who feel themselves pushed to the wall will naturally satisfy themselves with a small section of life, since they are foreign to life, and cannot see its problems with as much clarity as those who are playing the game according to the rules. They make bad teammates. They will not be so capable of understanding the finer things of life. Because of their very limited interest in living, they perceive but an insignificant segment of its problems for the reason that they fear a broader view would be synonymous with a loss of personal power. As to individual occurrences in life, we can often discover that an individual knows nothing of his capabilities of living, because he undervalues himself. We will find also that he is not sufficiently oriented concerning his short-comings; he will consider himself a good man, whereas in reality, he does everything out of egoism; or vice-versa, he will consider himself an egoist in instances in which a closer analysis shows him to be a very good person indeed. It really does not matter what you think of yourself, or what other people think of you. The important thing is the general attitude toward human society, since this determines every wish and every interest and every activity of each individual.

We are dealing again with two types of human beings. In the first class are those who live a more conscious life, who approach the problems of life without blinders on their eyes, in an objective manner. The second-class approaches life with a prejudiced attitude, and sees only a small part of it. The behavior and speech of individuals of this type are always directed in an unconscious manner. Two human beings living with one another may find difficulties in life because one of them is constantly in opposition. This is not an uncommon occurrence. It is perhaps even less uncommon that both parties are in opposition. Each party knows nothing about his opposition, believes himself right, and gives arguments to show that he is the champion of peace and harmony. The facts nevertheless belie his words. In actuality it is impossible for him to say a single word without attacking his partner on the flank with an opposing remark, albeit his attack is externally unnoticeable. On closer inspection we find that he has given himself up to a hostile and belligerent attitude throughout his life.

Human beings develop powers in themselves which are constantly at work, though they know nothing of them. These faculties lie hidden in the unconscious, influence their lives and occasionally lead to bitter consequences when they are not discovered. Dostoyevsky described such a case so beautifully in his novel *"The Idiot"* that it has been the marvel of psychologists ever since: during a social gathering a lady cautions the duke who is the hero of the novel, not to upset an expensive Chinese vase which stands near him, in a taunting tone. The duke assures her that he will take care, but a few minutes later the vase lies on the ground, shattered into pieces. No one in the group saw a mere accident in this occurrence; everyone felt it was a very consequent action, quite in keeping with the whole character of this man who felt himself insulted by the lady's words.

In judging a human being we must not be guided solely by his conscious actions and expressions. Often little details in his thinking and behavior of which he is not conscious will give us a better clue to his real nature.

People for instance who practice such unpleasant activities as nail-biting or nose-boring do not know that they betray the fact that they are stubborn human beings in doing so, since they do not understand the relationships which have led them to these traits. Yet it is perfectly clear to us that a child must have been scolded repeatedly because of these habits; if, then, he does not give them up, despite the scoldings, he must be a stubborn human being! Were we more expert in our observation, we would have to draw very far-reaching conclusions concerning any human being, by watching for such insignificant details, in which his whole being is mirrored.

These two following cases will show how important it is to the psychic economy that events which are unconscious, remain in the unconscious. The human soul has the capability of directing the consciousness, that is, of making conscious that which is necessary from the standpoint of some psychic movement, and vice-versa, to allow something to remain in the unconscious or make it unconscious, whenever this would seem advisable for the maintenance of the individual's behavior pattern.

The first case is that of a young man, a firstborn son, who grew up with a younger sister; his mother died when he was ten years old, and from that time his father, who was a very intelligent, well-meaning, ethical man, had to be the educator. The father spent most of his efforts developing his son's ambition and spurring him on to greater activity. The boy tried to be the leader in his classes, developed himself extraordinarily well, and so far as his ethical and scientific qualities were concerned, always took first place, muck to the joy of his father, who expected him to play an important role in life, from the very first.

In the course of time this young man developed certain traits which caused his father sorrow, and these he tried to change. The boy's sister grew up to be his obdurate rival. She also developed very well, although she was satisfied with utilizing the weapons of weakness for her triumphs, while she enlarged her significance at the cost of her brother. She had acquired a considerable facility in household talks, which made competition difficult for her brother. As a boy, he found it very difficult to achieve, in domesticity, that recognition and significance which he had so easily won in other fields of endeavor. The father soon noticed that his son was acquiring a peculiar social life, which became the more evident as his puberty approached. As a matter of fact, he had no social life. He was hostile to all new acquaintanceships and where these acquaintanceships concerned girls, he simply ran away. At first his father saw nothing extraordinary in this, but as time went on the boy's social reactions acquired such dimensions that he hardly went out of the house, and even little walks, except in the late twilight, were unpleasant to him. He became so shut in that he refused, finally, to greet even his old acquaintances, although his attitude in school and towards his father remained beyond criticism.

When it had gone so far that no one could bring him anywhere, the father brought this boy to the physician. A few consultations sufficed to discover the cause of the difficulty. This boy believed that his ears were small and that therefore everyone considered him very ugly. As a matter of fact, this was not the case. When his objection was overruled and he was told that his ears were in nowise different from those of other boys, and it was shown him that he was using this as an excuse to withdraw from the company of human beings, he added further that his teeth and his hair also were ugly. This also was not the case.

On the other hand, it was easily discovered that he was inordinately ambitious. He was well aware of his ambition and believed that his father, who had constantly stimulated him to greater and greater activity so that he might achieve a high position in life, had produced this trait in him. His plans for the future came to their climax in his desire to play the role of a hero of science. This would not be so remarkable were it not that with it was combined a tendency to avoid all the obligations of humanity and fellowship. Why did this boy make use of such very childish arguments? Had these arguments been right they might have justified him in approaching life with a certain caution and anxiety, because it is undoubtedly true that an ugly man encounters many difficulties in our civilization.

Further examination showed that this boy followed a particular goal with his great ambition. Formerly he had always been the first one in his class and he wanted to remain the first one. To achieve such a goal, one has certain instruments such as concentration, industry and the like, at hand. These were not enough for him. He attempted to exclude everything which seemed unnecessary, out of his life. He might have expressed himself somewhat like this: "Since I am going to become famous and since I am going to dedicate myself entirely to my scientific labors, I must exclude all social relationships as unnecessary."

But he neither said nor thought this. On the contrary he took the unessential element of his alleged ugliness and utilized it for the attainment of his purpose. The elevation of this insignificant fact acquired value in his scheme of things in that it justified him in doing what in reality he wanted to do. All he needed to do now was to have courage to argue falsely, to exaggerate his ugliness, in order to pursue his secret purpose. Had he said that he wished to live like an ascetic hermit in order to attain his goal of being the first, his argument would have been transparent to everyone. Although unconsciously he was dedicated to the idea of playing the heroic role, he was consciously unaware of his purpose.

That he wished to hazard everything else in life and gain this one point had never entered his head. If he had taken this into his consciousness and decided openly to stake everything in life in order to become a scientific hero, he could not have been as sure of himself as if he were to accomplish his purpose by saying that he was an ugly man and dared not go into society; in addition anyone who would say openly that he wanted forever to be first and the greatest, and was willing to sacrifice all human relationships for the sake of his goal, would make himself ridiculous in the eyes of his fellows. It would be too fearful a thought, a thought which one dared not think. There are certain ideas which one cannot hold too openly, both for the sake of others and for the sake of oneself. For this reason, the guiding idea of this boy's life had to remain in his unconscious.

If now we make obvious to such an individual the mainsprings of his life and demonstrate to him tendencies which he dared not look at in himself lest he lose his behavior pattern, we naturally disturb his entire psychic mechanism. What this individual has been trying at all costs to prevent, now happens! His unconscious thought processes become clear and transparent! Thoughts which were not to be thought, ideas which one dared not retain, tendencies which, if conscious, would disturb our entire behavior, are laid bare. It is a universal and human phenomenon that everyone seizes upon those thoughts which justify him in his attitude and rejects every idea which might prevent him from going on. Human beings dare only those things which in their interpretation of the world are valuable to them. That which is helpful we are conscious of; whatever can disturb our arguments we push into the unconscious.

The second case is the history of a very capable young boy whose father, a teacher, constantly spurred his son on to be the first in his class. In this case, too, the early days of this child were a series of victories. Wherever he appeared he was always the conqueror. He was one of the most charming members of his society and he had several dose friends.

A great change occurred in his eighteenth year. He lost all his pleasure in life, was depressed, distracted, and went to great lengths to withdraw from the world. No sooner would he make a friendship than he broke it. Everyone found a stumbling block in his behavior. His father however hoped that his shut-in life would enable him to dedicate himself more intensely to his studies.

During the treatment of this boy he complained constantly that his father had robbed him of all joy in life, that he could find no self-confidence nor courage to go on with life, and that there was nothing left for him to do but to sorrow through the rest of his days in solitude. His progress in his studies had already become slower and he was failing in college. He explained that the change in his life had begun on the occasion during a social gathering in which his ignorance of modern literature had made him the object of ridicule among his friends. The repetition of similar experiences caused him to begin his isolation and gave him occasion to assume a position outside society. He was ruled by the idea that his father was to blame for his misfortune, and their relationship became worse day by day.

These two cases are similar to each other in many respects. In the first case our patient was shipwrecked on the resistance of his sister, whereas in the second it was the belligerent attitude toward a father who was at fault. Both patients were led on by an idea which we have been accustomed to call the heroic ideal. Both of them had become so intoxicated with their heroic ideal that they had lost all contact with life, had become discouraged and would have liked nothing better than to withdraw entirely from the struggle. But we cannot believe that our second boy would ever have said to himself: "Since I cannot continue this heroic existence I shall withdraw from life and embitter the rest of my days!"

To be sure, his father was wrong and his education was bad. It was quite evident that he had eyes for nothing but his bad education, of which he constantly complained, since he wanted to justify himself in his withdrawal, by assuming that his education had been so bad that withdrawal from society alone remained a solution of his problem. In this way he achieved a situation in which he suffered no more defeats, and he was able to credit his father with the total blame for his misfortune. Only in this way was he able to save a fraction of his self-esteem for himself and satisfy his striving for significance. He had a glorious past and his future triumphs had been stopped only by the fatal fact that his father, because of his bad pedagogy, had hindered him from developing to even more brilliant accomplishments.

In a way we might say that something like this train of thought remained unconsciously in his mind: "Since I now stand closer to the firing front of life, and since I realize that it will no longer be so easy always to be the first, I shall make every effort to withdraw entirely from life." Yet such an idea is dearly unthinkable. No one could say such a thing, but an individual can act as if he had taken this thought to heart. This is accomplished by making use of still further arguments; by busying himself entirely with the educational mistakes of his father he succeeds in evading society and avoids all necessary decisions in life. Had this train of thought become conscious to him his secret behavior would, of necessity, have been disturbed. Therefore, it remained unconscious. How could anyone say that he was an untalented human being when he had such a glorious past? To be sure none could blame him now if he succeeded to no new triumphs! The pernicious influence of his father's educational efforts was not to be laid aside. The son was judge, claimant, and defendant all in his own person. Should he now give up such a favorable position? He knew too well that his father was to blame only so long as he, the son, wanted it, so long as he plied the lever which he held between his hands.

V. Dreams

It has long been maintained that one could draw conclusions concerning the personality-as-a-whole from the dreams of an individual. Lichtenberg, a contemporary of Goethe, once said that one could guess the character and essence of a human being better from his dreams than from his actions and words. This is saying a little too much. We have the standpoint that one must utilize *single* phenomena of the psychic life with the greatest care and only in connection with other phenomena. We therefore will draw conclusions concerning his character from the dreams of an individual only when we can find additional supporting evidence in other characteristics, to substantiate our interpretation of the dream.

The interpretation of dreams dates from prehistoric times. The research of various epochs in the developmental history of culture, especially as evidenced in myths and sagas, leads us to the conclusion that in times by-gone people were far more concerned with the interpretation of dreams than we are today. We also find a much better understanding of dreams on the part of the average man of those days than is the case today. One need but recall the enormous role of dreams in the life of the ancient Greeks, or the fact that Cicero wrote a book about them or remind oneself of the many dreams told in the Bible, to prove this point. And more. The Bible dreams are either cleverly interpreted, or they are related as though it were self-understood that everyone would then interpret them correctly and understand them. This is the case in the instance of Joseph's dream of the sheaves which he told his brothers. In the Nibelungen sagas, which originated in an entirely different culture, furthermore, we can conclude that dreams were used as evidence.

If we busy ourselves with dreams as a means of approaching and learning something of the human soul, we shall hardly view the problem from the standpoint of those investigators who seek in the dream and in dream interpretation fantastic and supernatural influences. We shall depend upon the evidence of dreams only when we can be justified and strengthened in our assertions by other far-reaching observations.

The tendency to believe that dreams have a particular meaning for the future, persists even today. There are idealists who go so far as to allow themselves to be influenced by their dreams. In this way one of our patients tricked himself into avoiding every honorable occupation and devoted himself to gambling on the Exchange. He always gambled according to dreams which he had. He had collected historical evidence to prove he had always had misfortune whenever he did not follow one of his dreams. To be sure, he would dream of nothing except that which was the object of his constant waking attention. In this way he patted himself on the back, so to speak, in his dream, and was enabled for a considerable period of time to say that he had won very much under the influence of his dream.

Sometime later he explained that he placed no value whatever upon his dreams. It seems that he had lost all his money. Since this happens frequently to stock market operators even without dreams, we see no miracle at work here. An individual who is intensely interested in some particular task is pursued by the necessity of solving this problem even at night. Some people do not sleep at all and constantly follow their problem while awake, others sleep but busy themselves with their plans in their dreams.

This peculiar phenomenon which occupies our thoughts during our sleep, is nothing more than the bridge from yesterday to tomorrow. If we know what attitude an individual takes towards life in general, how he bridges from the "now" into the "then," as a rule we will be able to understand also the peculiarities of his bridge structure in his dreams and be able to make valid conclusions from it. In other words, it is the general attitude toward life which is at the basis of all dreams.

A young woman has the following dream: she dreams that her husband has forgotten her wedding anniversary and she reproaches him for it. This dream may mean several things. If such a problem can occur at all it immediately shows us that this marriage is marked by certain difficulties; the wife feels herself neglected. She explains however that she also forgot about the wedding anniversary, but it was she who finally remembered it whereas her husband had to be reminded of it by her. She is the "better half." To a further question she said that actually nothing like this has ever happened and that her husband has always remembered the wedding anniversary. Therefore, in the dream we see her tendency to be anxious for the future; something like this might happen. We can further conclude that she is given to making reproaches, to using arguments which are intangible, and to nagging her husband for things which *might* occur.

Still we could not be sure of our interpretation if we did not have other evidence at hand which would reinforce our conclusions. Asked about her earliest childhood remembrance, this woman narrated an event which had always remained in her memory. When she was a three-year old child her aunt presented her with a carved wooden spoon of which she was very proud; but once as she was playing with it, it fell in a brook and floated away. She sorrowed about this event for many days in such a way that everyone in her environment was concerned with it.

The dream might lead us to assume that she was now again thinking of the possibility that her marriage also might float away from her. What if her husband *should* forget about her wedding anniversary?

Another time she dreamt that her husband led her up into a high building; the stairs grow more and more steep. Thinking that she has perhaps climbed too high she becomes terribly dizzy, has an attack of anxiety, and faints. One may experience a similar sensation during the waking life, especially if one suffers from dizziness in high places in which the fear is less that of the height than of the depth. By connecting the second dream with the first one and melting them together the thought, feeling, and content of these dreams give a clear impression that this is a woman who is anxious about falling, who is afraid of mischief or calamity. We can imagine that the waning affection of her husband, or something similar, would be such a calamity. What would happen if her husband in some way were not compatible? What if their married life were disturbed?

Scenes might occur, fights take place, which might end with the wife's fainting as though lifeless. This actually occurred once during a family argument!

Now we come nearer to the meaning of the dream. It is quite a matter of indifference in which material the thought and emotional content of the dreams express itself, or what instruments are used for this expression, so long as the material is in any way useful and *some* expression is assured. In the dream the life problem of an individual is expressed in a simile. It is as though she said, "Do not climb too high so that you will not fall too far!" It may be well to recall the reproduction of a dream in the "Marriage Song" of Goethe. A knight comes home from the country and finds his castle deserted. Tired out he falls into his bed and in his dream, he sees little figures coming out from under his bed and notices a marriage ceremony among these dwarfs. He is agreeably pleased by his dream. It is as though he wanted to corroborate in his thoughts the need for finding a woman. What he saw here in miniature occurred later in reality as he celebrated his own marriage.

We find many well-known elements in this dream. In the first place the preoccupation of the poet with his own marriage is hidden behind it. We can see further how the dreamer, in his utter need strikes an attitude toward his contemporary situation in life. This situation demands marriage. He occupies himself in his dream with the problem of marriage and on the following day decides that it would be better if he too, were to get married.

Now let us consider a dream of a twenty-eight-year-old man. The movement of the dream, changing from ascent to descent like the temperature curve of a fever, indicates very clearly the psychic movements with which the life of this man is filled. The feeling of infe-riority from which arise the tendencies and strivings for power and for dominance are easily recognized. He relates: "I am making an excursion with a large group of people. We must get out at a waystation because the ship on which we are to make this excursion is too small, and we must stay in this town overnight. During the night the report comes that the ship is sinking, and all participants in the excursion are called to man the pumps in order to prevent it. I remember that I have some valuables in my baggage and rush to the ship where everyone else is already working at the pumps. I seek to escape this work and look for the baggage room. I succeed in fishing my knapsack through the window and at the same time I see a penknife which I like very much next to my knapsack. I put it in the knapsack. With an acquaintance I jump off as the ship sinks deep-er and deeper. We jump off into the sea and land on the ground. Since the pier is too high, we wander fur-ther along and come to a precipitous cliff down which I must go. I slide down. I have not seen my companion since leaving the ship. I go faster and faster and fear that I will be killed. Finally, I land at the bottom and fall just in front of an acquaintance. It is an otherwise unknown young man who had been in a strike and had worked very quietly among the strikers, who was agreeable to me. He greets me with reproachful words, just as though he knew that I had left the others on the ship in the lurch. 'What are *you* doing here?' he asks. I seek to escape from this abyss which is surrounded on all sides by precipitous cliffs from which ropes hang down. I do not dare use them because they are too thin. With every attempt to climb out of the abyss I always slide back again. Finally, I am on top, but I don't know how I got there. It seems to me that I purposely did not want to dream this part of the dream, as if I wanted to skip over it impatiently. On the edge of the abyss, on top, there was a road which was protected on the side of the abyss by a fence. People were going by here and greeted me in a friendly fashion."

If we go back into the life of this dreamer the first thing that we hear is that he constantly suffered from severe illness up to the fifth year of his life, and that after this time he was often ill. As a result of his weak health he was carefully and anxiously guarded by his parents. His contact with other children was very slight. When he wanted to make contact with grownups, he was always told by his parents that children should be seen and not heard, and that children do not belong with adults. He thus failed at a very early age to find those points of contact which are necessary for social life and remained in connection solely with his parents. The further outcome of this was that he remained considerably behind his companions of the same age, with whom he could not keep up. We are not to be astonished to hear that he was also considered stupid among them, and soon became the butt of all their jokes. This circumstance, again, prevented him from finding friends.

An extraordinary feeling of inferiority was accentuated to the highest degree by these circumstances. His education was directed entirely by his well-wishing, but very irascible, military father, and by his weak, uncomprehending, very domineering mother. Although his parents were constantly reiterating their good will, his education must have been a very strict one. His discouragement played a considerable role in this process. A very significant event retained in his earliest childhood remembrances was that when he was but three years old his mother made him kneel an peas for half an hour. The reason for this was a disobedience whose cause his mother knew very well, as the child had told her. He had become frightened of a horseman and had therefore refused to run an errand for his mother. As a matter of fact he was spanked very seldom, but when this did occur, he was always beaten 83 Understanding Human Nature with a many-tailed dog whip, and never without being under the necessity of afterwards begging for forgiveness and relating the causes for which he had been beaten. "The child should know," said the father, "how he has misbehaved." Once he was beaten unjustly and as he could not say afterwards why he was beaten, was beaten again, indeed was beaten until he confessed to some misdeed or other.

A belligerent feeling towards his parents was present from his earliest days. His feeling of inferiority had acquired such dimensions that he could not even conceive of being superior. His life at school as well as at home was an almost unbroken chain of greater or lesser defeats. The smallest victory, in his opinion, was denied him, At school, up to the time that he was eighteen years old, he was always the one who was laughed at. Once he was laughed at even by his teacher, who read a bad theme aloud to the class and accompanied the reading with derisive remarks.

Everyone of these occurrences forced him further and further into isolation, and sooner or later he began to withdraw from the world, of his own accord. In his battle with his parents he happened upon a very effective although costly method of attack. He refused to speak, and with this gesture, he relinquished the most important grappling hook with which one fastens himself to the outer world. Since he was unable to speak with anyone, he became entirely solitary. Misunderstood by all, he spoke to none, particularly not with his parents; and finally no one addressed him Every attempt to bring him into society came to grief, as every attempt to establish love relationships later in his life also failed, much to his sorrow. This is the course of his life until his twenty-eighth year. The deep inferiority complex which had permeated his whole spirit had as a consequence given rise to an ambition beyond all reason, an unreined striving for significance and superiority which ceaselessly distorted his feeling of human fellowship. The less he spoke, the more was his psychic life filled, by day and by night, with dreams of triumphs and victories of every sort.

And thus, he dreamt one night the dream which we have related above, in which we see clearly the movement and the pattern according to which his psychic life developed. In conclusion let us recall a dream which Cicero has related, one of the most famous prophetic dreams in literature.

The poet Simonides, who at one time had found the corpse of an unidentified man lying on the street and had cared for his decent interment, was warned by the ghost of this old dead man, as he was about to attempt a sea journey, that if he should take the journey he would be shipwrecked. Simonides did not go and all those who did, died.[1]

According to the report this event in connection with the dream is supposed to have had an unusually deep impression on all people for hundreds of years.

If we want to interpret this occurrence we must maintain that in that time ships were wrecked very

1   Cf. Enne Nielson, "The Unexplained, In Its Course Through The Centuries." Published by the Langewies che-Brandt. Ebenhausen near Munich

frequently, and also that because of this reason many people who were on the eve of a sea journey, dreamt of shipwrecks, and that among these many dreams this particular dream demonstrated a particular coincidence between dream and reality which was so remarkable that it remained for posterity. It is quite conceivable that those who have a tendency to ferret out mysterious relationships have an especial weakness for just such stories, whereas we very calmly and soberly interpret the dream as follows: our poet probably never showed any great desire to take this trip because of his considerable care for his bodily well-being; as the hour of decision neared he was hard put to it to find a justification for his hesitating attitude. For this reason, he allowed the corpse who was under the necessity of proving himself grateful for his decent burial, to appear in a prophetic role. That he now did not take the trip is self-understood. If the ship had not gone under the world would never have learned about the dream nor the story, in all probability. For we experience only those things which set our brain into unrest, which demonstrate to us that there is more wisdom hidden between heaven and earth than we allow ourselves to dream of. We can understand the prophetic nature of dreams in so far as we know that both dream and reality contain the same attitude toward life which an individual shows.

Another thing which we must consider is the fact that all dreams are not so easily understood; as a matter of fact only a very few are. We forget the dream immediately after it has left its peculiar impression and do not understand what is behind it unless we have been versed in the interpretation of dreams. Yet these dreams, too, are but a symbolic and metaphoric reflection of the activity and behavior pattern of an individual. The main meaning of a simile or comparison is that it affords us access to a situation in which we are anxious to find ourselves. If we are occupied with the solution of a problem and if our personality points a specific direction of approach, then we need but seek for an animating push to propel us into it. The dream is extraordinarily well suited to intensify an emotion or produce the verve which is necessary to the, solution of a particular situation. Nothing is altered by the fact that the dreamer does not understand the connection. It suffices that he finds the material and the boost in some fashion; the dream itself will give evidence of the manner in which the thought processes of the dreamer express themselves, as it will indicate the behavior pattern of the dreamer. The dream is like a column of smoke which shows that a fire is burning somewhere. The experienced woodsman can observe the smoke and tell what kind of wood is burning, just as the psychiatrist can draw conclusions concerning the nature of an individual by interpreting his dream.

Summing up, we can say that a dream shows not only that the dreamer is occupied in the solution of one of his life's problems, but also how he approaches these problems. In particular, those two factors which influence the dreamer in his relation- ship with the world and reality, the social feeling and the striving for Power, will make themselves evident in his dream.

VI. Talent

Among those psychic phenomena which enable us to judge an individual we have left out of consideration one which is concerned with his intellectual powers.

We have placed little value upon what an individual says or thinks of himself. We are convinced that each of us can somehow go astray and that each of us feels himself under the necessity of retouching his psychic image for his fellow man, through various of the complicated egoistic, moral, or other tricks. One thing we are, however, permitted to do, and that is to draw certain conclusions from specific thought processes and their expression in speech, even though this is possible only to a limited degree. We cannot exclude thought and speech from our examination if we wish to judge the individual correctly.

What we are pleased to call talent, that is the special ability to make judgments, has been the subject of numerous observations, analyses, and tests, among which the tests of intelligence, in children and adults, are well known. These are the so-called tests for talent. Up to the present time these tests have been unsuccessful. Whenever a number of pupils are tested the results usually show what the teacher could easily have determined without tests. In the beginning the experimental psychologists were very proud of this although it must have been evident at the same time that the tests were, to a certain degree, superfluous. Another objection to intelligence tests is the fact that the thought and judgment processes and abilities of children do not develop regularly, so that many children who show poor results on the tests, suddenly show an extraordinarily good development and talent after a few years. Another element which must be considered is that children in large cities, and those from certain social circles, are better prepared for the tests by virtue of their broader life. Their seemingly greater intelligence is deceptive and places other children who have not such a fund of preparation, relatively in the shadow. It is well known that eight- to ten-year-old children of well-to-do families, are much more quick witted than poor children of the same age. This does not mean that the children of the wealthy are more talented but that the cause for this difference lies entirely in the circumstances of their previous life.

Up to the present time we have not gone very far with tests of talent, as is very evident when we view the sorry results which have been shown in Berlin and Hamburg where those children who evinced the greatest talent in the tests failed in conspicuous percentages later on in their education. This phenomenon would seem to prove that we have no certain guarantee for the future healthy development of the child in the results of his mental test. The experiments of Individual Psychology, quite on the contrary, have stood the test far better, because they have not been directed toward the determination of a particular degree of development, but rather have been designed to further the understanding of the positive factors underlying this development. These same observations have, when necessary, pressed the proper instruments of correction into the hands of the child. It has been the principle of Individual Psychology never to dissolve the thought and judgment powers of a child out of the structure of his soul life, but to view them solely in connection with his other psychic processes.

9 786257 836418